Scottish Wit & Wisdom

The Meanings Behind Famous Scottish Sayings

Betty Kirkpatrick

Crombie Jardine
PUBLISHING LIMITED

4, Belgrave Place
Edinburgh
EH4 3AN
www.crombiejardine.com

This edition was first published by
Crombie Jardine Publishing Limited in 2007,
ISBN-13 978-1-906051-13-6

Published by Crombie Jardine Publishing Limited
in paperback in 2005,
ISBN-10 1-905102-07-0

Printed & bound in China

did not recognize wit when it was presented to them.

There is less need to explain the wisdom of the Scots, since Scotland, especially considering its size, has produced a great number of people who have made a significant contribution to the shaping of the world. These have included people from a wide range of disciplines, such as poets, philosophers, novelists, artists, architects, engineers,

explorers, doctors, scientists and
so on, and the thoughts of some
of these are included in the
following selection of sayings
and quotations.

Any collection of these,
especially such a short one,
is bound to be extremely
personal and I have decided
to concentrate on the
traditional and the historical.
In this modern age where so
much is disposable and so

ephemeral, it is good, I think, to give prominence, at least occasionally, to the tried and the true.

The Scots have their own language that developed quite separately from English, although they share a common ancestor in Old English. Over the centuries, however, for various political, educational and cultural reasons, English gradually became the dominant language in Scotland, and now, though valiant efforts are being made to revive the flagging spirit of the Scots language, there are many people, especially of the younger generation, who know, at best, only a few words of it. Thus, although several of the traditional sayings in proverbs contain Scots words, these are absent from many of the quoted writers because they penned their thoughts in English.

A short glossary has been added as a guide to the Scots element in the book. In case you are puzzled over any of the spellings of Scots words, it should be remembered that Scots, unlike English and most other languages, lacks a standard spelling scheme. This inevitably gives rise to one word having several variants, making it almost impossible to misspell a Scots word.

SAGE SAYINGS & PITHY PROVERBS

HEALTH

Better wear shoon than sheets.
It is better to wear shoes to keep the feet warm and dry (even though this may be expensive) rather than become ill.

A cauld needs the cook as muckle as the doctor.
Nutritious food can cure a cold as effectively as medicine.

Feed a cauld and starve a fever.

Traditional advice about giving nutritious food to people suffering with a cold is not always appropriate if they have a fever.

Feed a cauld but hunger a colic.

A similar sentiment to the previous saying, where the condition not requiring nourishment is a stomach disorder.

Fill fu' and haud fu' maks a stark man.

Plenty of good food and drink makes a person strong.

Gae tae bed wi' the lamb and rise wi' the laverock.

A recipe for remaining healthy; a Scots version of 'early to bed, early to rise'.

He that eats but ae dish
seldom needs the doctor.
*A warning to be sparing in the
amount of food you eat, if you
want to remain healthy.*

If ye want to be soon
weel be lang sick.
*Not a recommendation to malinger,
but advice not to get out of bed too
soon after you have been ill.*

Licht suppers mak lang days.
*A recommendation to eat sparingly,
especially in the evening, if you wish
to live to an old age.*

Rise when the day daws,
Bed when the nicht fa's.
*An injunction to stay healthy by going to
bed early and getting up early.*

Suppers kill
mair than doctors cure.
*Another recommendation to eat sparingly,
especially in the evening.*

FOOD

A drap and a bit's
but sma' requite.

*Said as an invitation to guests to partake of
food and drink, indicating that this is little
recompense for their friendship.*

A hungry man's an angry man.
This speaks for itself – it is undoubtedly true that many people become bad-tempered when they get hungry.

A hungry man's meat is lang o' makin' ready.
When you're very hungry the preparation of your food seems to take a very long time; a similar saying to 'a watched pot never boils'.

A hungry wame has nae lugs.
Those who are hungry seem to lose the power of hearing and so don't listen to reason.

A kiss and a drink o' watter mak a wersh breakfast.

Said as a warning to a couple who think they can live on love and very little else.

As the soo fills, the draff soors.

Literally, as the sow fills up, its food begins to taste sour; a compliment to a host to express that the food has been so plentiful and so good that the guest's appetite has been fully satisfied and he/she can eat no more.

Bannocks are better than nae breid.

Very plain food is better than no food at all; a similar saying to 'half a loaf is better than no bread'.

Better belly burst than gude meat spoil.

It is better to eat too much than let good food go to waste; said by those who eat too much, as justification for their greed.

Better wait on the cook than the doctor.

A reference to the fact that many people felt that the ill would benefit more from nourishing food than medicine, although this could vary with the type of illness.

Breid's hoose is skailed never.

If a house contains bread you can never say it has no food in it.

Eat in measure and defy the doctor.

Moderation in eating makes for a healthy life.

Eats meat, an's never fed;
wears claes and never cled.
No matter how well-fed or well-clothed
some people may be, they never seem to
look any better for it.

Eat weel's drink weel's brither.
Eating well and drinking well
should go together.

Fat paunches bode lean pows.
People who are greedy and over-fed
have empty heads.

Hunger's good kitchen.

When you're hungry any food tastes good.

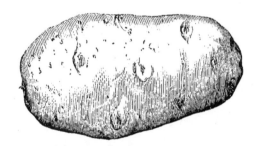

Hunger's good kitchen to a cauld potato, but a wet divot to the lowe o' love.

Hunger makes the humblest of food (such as a cold potato) seem very appetizing, but it dampens romantic passion.

I'm neither sma' drink thirsty nor grey bread hungry.

Said by someone who is disappointed at the standard of fare that he/she has been offered by a host.

Mennans are better than nae meat.

Both this and the saying opposite indicate that it is better to have very little food than no food at all. In Scots the word meat is often used for food in general and mennans are minnows or very small fish.

Poor folk seek meat for their stamacks and rich folk seek stamacks for their meat.

The poor eat because they're hungry, the rich because they feel they have to, even if they have little appetite.

Mennans are better than nae fish.

See the saying on the previous page.

Naething sooner maks
a man auld-like than
fitting ill to his meat.
*Nothing ages people so rapidly
as being ill-fed.*

Ne'er gie' me death
in a toom dish.
*A jocular saying used by people who like
their food and want some of it, literally
meaning 'don't give me death by means of
an empty dish, don't starve me to death'.*

Ne'er speak ill o' them
whose breid ye eat.
A warning not to criticize your host.

O' a' the meat in the warld, the
drink gaes best doon.
*This speaks for itself in a land that
makes and loves whisky.*

Some hae meat and canna eat
And some wad meat that want it
But we hae meat and we can eat,
For which the Lord be thankit.
A grace said before meals, known
as the Selkirk Grace.

They may ken by your beard
what has been on your board.
A way of telling someone that some of
the food he has just eaten is stuck
on his beard or chin.

The nearer the grave, the greedier.

The older people get, the more food they like to have.

Stuffin' hauds oot storms.

Advice given to people who are setting out on a journey in bad weather to eat well before they leave.

Welcome's the best dish
in the kitchen.
Food given with a good will tastes the best.

They hae need o'a canny
cook that hae but ae egg to
their denner.
*It takes a clever, ingenious cook to make
a meal out of very little; also extended to
mean that it takes a resourceful person to
make the most of what is to hand.*

Tak a piece – your teeth's
longer than your beard.
*Words of encouragement said to
children to get them to take a titbit or
treat when they have the chance.*

⊕

Ye hae tint your ain stamack
an' found a tyke's.
*A remark made to someone who is eating a
great deal as though very hungry.*

⊕

Your meat will mak you bonny
and when you're bonny you'll
be well lo'ed and when you're
well lo'ed you'll be licht-hearted
and when you're licht-hearted
you'll loup far.

Said to children to encourage them to eat.

What's in your wame's no in
your testament.

*Said as an encouragement to someone
to eat up; a reminder that if you eat
everything on your plate you cannot leave
it to someone else in your will.*

35

When all fruit fa's,
welcome ha's.

*When we have consumed all the finer food,
we must be content with the plain kind.*

WEATHER

About the moon there is a brough,
The weather will be cold and rough.
A warning of rough weather if there is a halo effect round the moon.

A green Yule maks
a fat kirkyard.
A wet winter results in many deaths because of the many illnesses that are caused or worsened by damp conditions.

As the day lengthens, the cauld strengthens.

A reminder that when the days begin to get longer, the weather often becomes colder.

Cast not a clout till May be oot.

Often taken to mean that people should not remove any of their winter clothing until the month of May has passed. However, it is thought by some that May refers to the hawthorn, the advice being not to remove any winter clothes until the hawthorn is in blossom.

East and wast
the sign o' a blast;
north and south,
the sign o' a drouth.

*A saying that uses the direction of the
prevailing wind to forecast the weather.*

E'ening grey
an' a morning
red, put on your
hat or ye'll wet
your head.
E'ening red an'
a morning grey,
is a taiken
o' a bonny day.
*A weather saying with
a similar meaning
to 'red sky at night,
shepherd's delight, red
sky in the morning,
shepherd's warning'.*

If Candlemas Day
be dry and fair
The hauf o' winter's
to come and mair.
If Candlemas Day
be wet and foul,
The hauf o' winter's
gaun at Yule.

*Candlemas Day is February 2
and it was taken as a good weather
sign if it was wet on that day.*

If grass grows green in Janaveer, it will be the waur for it a' the year.

The belief was that if the grass was green too early in the year, it was unlikely to survive the rest of the year.

Mony haws, mony snaws.

A warning that a good harvest of haw berries will result in a cold, hard winter.

Mist in May and heat in June
make the harvest right soon.
A self-evident weather saying.

Sorrow an' ill
weather come unca'd.
*Both ill fortune and ill weather
are beyond our control.*

44

The rain cams scouth, when the wind's i' the south.

In this context scouth means freely, without restraint, and so the saying indicates that heavy rain will occur when there a wind blowing from the south.

When the moon is on her back Gae mend your shoon and sort your thack.

When the moon appears in such a position, it should be seen as a sign of rain, and appropriate measures should be taken.

Under water dearth, under snaw bread.

A field that has been flooded with water will produce a very poor crop, but one that has been covered in snow will produce a good one.

46

MONEY

A' complain o' want o' siller,
but nane o' want o' sense.
A saying indicating that desiring more
money is a far more common human
preoccupation than desiring more sense.

❋

A deaf man
will hear the
clink o' money.
A saying that emphasizes the
lure of money very well.

❋

Get what you can,
and keep what you hae,
that's the way to get rich.
*It sounds so easy that it makes
you wonder why there are not
more rich people around!*

A fu' sack can
bear a clout i'
the side.
*A prosperous person can afford
to take a few knocks from fate.*

Better a tocher in her than wi' her.

A tocher was a woman's dowry and this saying suggests that it was better for a woman to have good qualities within, rather than have a lot of money and possessions.

Gathering gear is weel-liket wark.

Acquiring money is generally thought to be a pleasant occupation.

He's got his nose in a gude kail pat.

Literally, he has got his head in a good soup pot; said of a person who has married someone well-off.

He wad rake hell for a bodle.

A saying indicating how much someone loves money and what a miser he is, a bodle being an old copper coin.

Eaten meat is ill to pay.
*No one likes to have to pay for something
that has already been consumed.*

**Lay your wame
to your winning.**
*A warning not to consume
more than you earn.*

**It's folly to live poor
to dee rich.**
*The moral is self-evident, akin to
'you can't take it with you'.*

Moyen does muckle,
but moyen does mair.
*Influence can do a lot,
but money is even
more powerful.*

There are nane sae
weel shod but may slip.
*Everyone, including the wealthy, is at risk
from misfortune and mishaps.*

He wad skin a
louse for the tallow.
*A saying that describes just
how miserly someone is.*

It's as easy to get siller frae a
lawyer as butter frae a black
dog's hause.

*Hause means throat in this instance, so the
saying suggests that acquiring silver from a
lawyer is an impossible feat.*

Wealth gars wits waver.
*People tend to lose their common sense
when money is involved.*

Wealth has made mair men covetous than covetousness has made men wealthy.
A warning against greed.

The siller penny slays mair souls than the nakit sword slays bodies.
*A comment on the destructive
power of money.*

Put twa pennies in a purse and they will creep thigither.

A saying indicating how money soon accumulates if you save it.

Want o' wit is waur than want o' gear.

It is worse to be lacking in intelligence and sense than to be lacking in money.

56

SILENCE

A close mou catches nae flees.

A recommendation to say as little as possible; a variation on 'shut your mouth and you'll get no flies'.

Ah dinna bile ma cabbages twice.

Said as a refusal to repeat what has just been said; literally 'I don't boil my cabbages twice'.

Dinna open yer mou tae fill ither fowks.

A warning not to gossip.

Gie yer tongue mair
holidays than yer heid.
*An imaginative way of suggesting that
people should think more than they speak.*

Keep yer mou shut
and yer een open.
*A warning that you will learn more if you
say little and observe a lot.*

Keep your breath tae
cool yer parritch.
*A piece of advice given to someone
who is wasting words.*

He that spares to speak, spares to speed.

A saying not in favour of silence, but one that suggests that people who don't point out their own talents don't succeed.

Keep yer gab steekit when ye kenna yer company.

A warning not to say too much in front of strangers; literally to keep your mouth closed when you don't know who is present.

Put your thoom on that!

Literally, put your thumb on that; said as a warning to keep something secret.

Pint stoups
hae lang lugs.
*A reminder that
those who drink
too much often say
too much.*

❖

The loodest bummer's
no the best bee.
*The person who says the most is rarely the
most effective person.*

When a' men speak,
nae man hears.

If everyone speaks at once, no one hears or takes in anything that is said.

Think mair than ye say.

Devote more time to thought than speech.

Wae is the wife that wants a tongue, but weel's the man that gat her.

It is unfortunate to be a woman who says very little, since little notice will be taken of her, but it is fortunate to be a man who marries such a woman.

Wide lugs
and a short
tongue
are best.
*It is best to listen
a lot and say
very little.*

64

TRUTH

A fu' heart never lied.
People are more likely to tell the truth when they are in the grip of emotion.

Auld saws speak truths.
There's a lot of truth in old sayings, as this collection proves.

Craft maun hae claes, but truth gangs nakit.
Cunning may be disguised, but truth does not need any cover or embellishment.

**Facts are chiels
that winna ding.**
*Facts, and therefore the truth,
cannot be denied.*

**He never lies,
but when the holly's green.**
*Since holly is an evergreen tree,
this saying indicates that the person in
question never tells the truth.*

If a'thing's true, that's nae lee.

A saying used to express disbelief in what has just been said.

It's a sin to lee on the diel.

You should always speak the truth, even where wicked people are concerned.

Truth and honesty keep the croon on the causey.

People who are honest and truthful stay out of trouble. The 'croon o' the causey' or the crown of the causeway was the highest part of the street, farthest way from the gutter where all the rubbish gathered.

Truth will stand when a'thing's failin'.

Truth can be relied upon when everything else fails.

WORDS

A' are no freens
that speak us fair.

*Just because someone pays you
a compliment or says something
nice about you, you cannot assume
that he/she is your friend.*

A' his buzz shaks nae barley.

*Said of someone who may say a
great deal but whose words have
no effect on the situation.*

A man o' words but no' o' deeds
is like a garden fu' o' weeds.
*A saying telling us that actions are much
more useful than mere words.*

Bairns speak i' the field whit
they hear i' the ha'.
*A warning to parents to be careful
what they say in front of their children
in case what was uttered in private
is repeated in public.*

Muckle spoken, part spilt.
*Said of a subject which has been talked
about to such an extent that much of its
meaning has been lost or ignored.*

Praise without profit
puts little i' the pat.
*Fine words alone are not much
practical use to anyone.*

Glib i' the tongue is aye
glaikit at the heart.
*Another saying that warns against being
impressed or taken in by the flattery of
smooth-talking people, as they are very
likely to be insincere.*

Words are but wind,
but dunts are the devil.
*Physical blows are much
worse than verbal abuse.*

Fair words winna
mak the pot boil.
*A saying that stresses the
inadequacy of mere words.*

Bees that hae honey in
their mouths hae stings
in their tails.

*A warning to be wary of people who are
particularly eloquent or flattering, as they
may be up to no good.*

There's a word in my wame,
but it's o'er far down.

*A saying used by someone to indicate that
he/she cannot think of the right word at
that moment; similar to having a word on
the tip of your tongue.*

Sticks and stanes may brak my banes, but names will never hurt me.

A saying indicating that, although physical abuse may do harm to someone, verbal insults will not; often used by schoolchildren to their tormentors.

Thanks winna feed the cat.

Verbal thanks is not worth much; sometimes said as a grudging, belittling acknowledgement of spoken thanks.

Ye wad wheedle a laverock frae the lift.

Said to someone who is particularly charming or persuasive, as though they are able to persuade the lark to leave the sky.

It's a gude tongue that says nae ill, but a better heart that thinks none.

A self-evident saying that praises the harbouring of charitable thoughts.

QUOTATIONS

JOHN LOGIE BAIRD (1888–1946)
television pioneer

◇◇◇◇◇◇◇◇◇◇◇◇◇◇◇◇◇◇◇◇◇◇◇◇◇◇◇◇◇◇◇◇◇◇

Seeing by wireless.
A definition of television ascribed to him

LADY FRANCES BALFOUR (1858–1931)
writer and suffragist

◇◇◇◇◇◇◇◇◇◇◇◇◇◇◇◇◇◇◇◇◇◇◇◇◇◇◇◇◇◇◇◇◇

Golf has ceased to be a peculiarly
national game. It is now no longer a
pastime for the impecunious Scot,
armed with two or three clubs,
and a feather ball, it has become
a professional sport, pursued by
devastating hordes of foreigners
among whom the American tongue
rises shrill and strident.

Ne Obliviscaris: Dinna Forget (1930)

J. M. BARRIE (1860–1937)
playwright and novelist

We are undoubtedly
a sentimental people,
and it sometimes plays
havoc with that other
celebrated sense of ours,
the practical.

From a speech to the Royal Scottish
Corporation on 30 November 1928

JAMES BOSWELL (1740–95)
biographer of Samuel Johnson

◇◇

We cannot tell the precise
moment when friendship is formed.
As in filling a vessel drop by drop,
there is at last a drop that makes it
run over; so in a series of kindnesses,
there is at last one which makes the
heart run over.

Life of Samuel Johnson (1791)

JOHN BUCHAN (1875–1940)
writer and statesman

◇◇◇◇◇◇◇◇◇◇◇◇◇◇◇◇◇◇◇◇◇◇◇◇◇◇◇◇◇◇◇◇◇

The dominant thought of youth
is the bigness of the world, of age
its smallness. As we grow older we
escape from the tyranny of matter
and recognize that the true centre of
gravity is the mind.

Memory Hold-the-Door (1941)

Robert Burns (1759–96)

poet and song-writer

Princes and lords are but the
breath of kings, 'An honest man's
the noblest work o' God'.

The Cotter's Saturday Night (1785) –
Burns quotes Alexander Pope

The best-laid schemes o' mice and men
Gang aft agley,
An' leave us nought but grief an' pain,
For promis'd joy!

To a Mouse (1785) –
oft-quoted lines commenting on the
essential fallibility of plans and hopes

Then gently scan your brother Man,
Still gentler sister woman,
Tho' they may gang a kennin' wrang,
To step aside is human.

Address to the Unco' Guid (1786) –
lines that urge people to refrain from passing
judgement on others

O wad some Power the giftie gie us
To see oursels as ithers see us!
It wad frae monie a blunder free us,
An' foolish notion.

To a Louse (1786) – a poem written when
he saw such a creature on a lady's hat in
church, with lines indicating that we would not
behave so foolishly if we could view ourselves
with the eyes of others

But pleasures are like poppies spread,
You seize the flower, its bloom is shed,
Or like the snow falls in the river,
A moment white – then melts forever.

Tam o' Shanter (1790) – lines indicating
that Burns could be lyrical in English as
well as Scots

Then let us pray that come it may,
As come it will, for a' that,
That sense and worth, o'er a' the earth'
Shall bear the gree, an a' that;
For a' that and a' that,
It's comin' yet for a' that,
That man to man the world o'er,
Shall brothers be for a' that.

For a' that and a' that (1795)

THOMAS CARLYLE (1795–1881)
historian and essayist

◇◇◇◇◇◇◇◇◇◇◇◇◇◇◇◇◇◇◇◇◇◇◇◇◇◇◇◇◇◇◇◇

In the long run every Government
is the exact symbol of its People,
with their wisdom and their
unwisdom; we have to say,
Like People like Government.

Past and Present (1843)

90

A well-written Life is almost as
rare as a well-spent one.

Critical and Miscellaneous Essays (1838)

If Jesus Christ were to come
today, people would not even crucify
him. They would ask him to dinner,
and hear what he had to say,
and make fun of it.

Carlyle at His Zenith (1927) by D. A. Wilson

ANDREW CARNEGIE (1835–1919)
industrialist and philanthropist

◇◇

There is an unwritten law among the best workmen: 'Thou shalt not take thy neighbour's job.'

Forum (August 1886)

Golf is an indispensable adjunct to high civilization.

Said when leaving a large sum of money to Yale University to build a golf course

LORD HENRY COCKBURN (1779–1854)
judge

◇◇◇◇◇◇◇◇◇◇

I never see a scene of Scotch
beauty, without being thankful
that I have beheld it before it has
been breathed over by the angel of
mechanical destruction.

Circuit Journeys (1847)

SIR ARTHUR CONAN DOYLE
(1859–1930)
novelist – creator of Sherlock Holmes

It is a capital mistake to theorize
before one has data. Insensibly one
begins to twist facts to suit theories,
instead of theories to suit facts.

A Scandal in Bohemia (1891)

SIR ALEXANDER FLEMING (1881–1955)
bacteriologist and discoverer of penicillin

This thirst for immediate results is
by no means uncommon, but it is
extremely harmful. Really valuable
research is a long-term affair.

The Life of Sir Alexander Fleming
(1959) by André Maurois

A good gulp of whisky at bedtime – it's
not very scientific, but it helps.

A remedy for the common cold ascribed to him

Sir Patrick Geddes (1854–1932)
townplanner and biologist

◇◇◇◇◇◇◇◇◇◇◇◇◇◇◇◇◇◇◇◇◇◇◇◇◇◇◇◇◇◇◇◇◇◇◇◇◇◇◇

When an idea is dead it is embalmed
in a textbook.

The Worlds of Patrick Geddes
(1978) by Philip Boardman

(James) Keir Hardie (1856–1915)
Labour politician

◇◇◇◇◇◇◇◇◇◇◇◇◇◇◇◇◇◇◇◇◇◇◇◇◇◇◇◇

I think it could be shown that the
position of women, as of most other
things, has always been better, nearer
to equality, with man, in Celtic, than
in non-Celtic, races.

DAVID HUME (1711–76)
philosopher and historian

The great end of all human industry
is the attainment of happiness.
For this were arts invented, science
cultivated, laws ordained and societies
modelled by the most profound
wisdom of patriots and legislators.

Essays: Moral, Political and Literary,
'The Stoic' (1742)

David Livingstone (1813–73)
missionary and explorer

◇◇◇

The strangest thing I have seen in this country seems really to be broken-heartedness and it attacks free men who have been captured and made slaves.

Last Journal of David Livingstone
in Central Africa (1874)

Hugh McDiarmid, pseudonym of Christopher Grieve (1892–1978)

poet

◇◇◇◇◇◇◇◇

There is so much that is bad in all
the poetry that Scots people know
and admire that it is not surprising that
for their pet example of a good
bad poet they should have to go outside
the range of poetry, good, bad, or
indifferent altogether. McGonagall is
in a very special category, and has it
entirely to himself.

Scottish Eccentrics (1936)

Charles Rennie Mackintosh
(1868–1928)
architect and designer

◇◇◇◇◇◇◇◇◇◇◇◇◇◇◇◇◇◇◇◇◇◇◇◇◇◇◇◇◇◇◇

Don't meddle with other people's ideas
when you have all the work cut out of
you in trying to express your own.

Seemliness (1902)

JOHN MUIR (1838–1914)
naturalist and founder of the American
Natural Park system

◇◇◇◇◇◇◇◇◇◇◇◇◇◇◇◇◇◇◇◇◇◇◇◇◇◇◇◇◇◇◇

Wherever a Scotsman goes, there goes
Burns. His grand whole, catholic soul
squares with the good of all; therefore
we find him in everything everywhere.

John of the Mountains
(1938), edited by I. M. Wolfe

Margaret Oliphant (1828–97)
novelist and critic

◇◇◇◇◇◇◇◇◇◇◇◇◇◇◇◇◇◇◇◇◇◇◇◇◇◇◇◇◇◇

Life is no definite thing with
a beginning and an end, a growth and
a climax; but a basket of fragments,
passages that lead to nothing, curious
incidents which look of importance
at first, but which crumble and break
into pieces, dropping into ruins.

Review of Henry James's *A London Life* in
Backwoods' Edinburgh Magazine (1888)

Sir Walter Scott (1771–1832)
novelist and poet

×××××××××××××××××××××××××××××××

Oh, what a tangled web we weave,
When first we practise to deceive!

Marmion (1808)

I make it a rule to cheat nobody
but booksellers, a race on whom
I have no mercy.

Letter to Thomas Sheridan (1811)

To live the life of an author
for mere bread is perhaps
the most dreadful fate than
can be encountered.

Letter to James Bailey (June 1817)

Many a clever boy is flogged
into a dunce and many an
original composition corrected
into mediocrity.

Journal (June 1826)

But who cares for the whipped
cream of London society?

Journal (April 1828)

Surely chess-playing is a sad
waste of brains.

Memoirs of the Life of Walter Scott
(1837–8) by J. G. Lockhart

SAMUEL SMILES (1812–1904)
social reformer and moralist

◇◇

That terrible Nobody!
How much has he to answer for.
More mischief is done by Nobody
than by all the world besides.

Thrift (1875)

ADAM SMITH (1723–90)
economist and philosopher

◇◇◇◇◇◇◇◇◇◇◇◇◇◇◇◇◇◇◇◇◇◇◇◇◇◇◇◇◇◇◇◇◇◇◇◇◇◇

It is not from the benevolence of the butcher, the brewer, or the baker, that we expect our dinner, but from their regard to their own interest.

An Inquiry into the Nature and Causes of the Wealth of Nations (1776)

ALEXANDER SMITH (1829–67)

poet

◇◇◇◇◇◇◇◇◇◇

It is not of so much consequence what
you say, as how you say it. Memorable
sentences are memorable on account
of some single irradiating word.

'On the Writing of Essays', Dreamthorp (1863)

TOBIAS SMOLLETT (1721–71)
novelist

◇◇◇◇◇◇◇◇◇◇◇◇

London is the devil's drawing-room.
The Adventures of Roderick Random (1748)

WILLIAM SOUTAR (1898–1943)
poet and diarist

◇◇◇◇◇◇◇◇◇◇◇◇◇◇◇◇◇◇◇◇◇◇◇

Life is no loving father, but a force
with which we must contend and to
which we must adapt the self.

Diary entry (June 1932)

Robert Louis Stevenson (1850–94)
novelist, poet and essayist

For my own part, I travel not to
go anywhere, but to go. I travel for
travel's sake.

Travels with a Donkey (1879)

From *Virginibus Puerisque* (1881):

Even if we take marriage at its
lowest, even if we regard it as no
more than a sort of friendship
recognized by the police.

You can read Kant by yourself if you wanted, but you must share a joke with someone else. Books are good enough in their own way, but they are a mighty bloodless substitute for life.

It is better to lose health like a spendthrift than to waste it like a miser. It is better to live and be done with it than to die daily in the sick room.

114

From *Memories and Portraits* (1887):

The first step for all is to
learn to the very dregs our own
ignoble fallibility. Faith means
holding the same opinions as the
person employing the word.

Marriage is one long
conversation, chequered
by disputes.

Scientific men, who imagine that their science affords an answer to the problem of existence, are perhaps the most to be pitied of mankind; and contemned.

To travel hopefully is a better thing than to arrive.

JAMES THOMSON (1700–48)

poet

◇◇◇◇◇◇◇◇◇◇

Poor is the triumph o'er the timid hare!

The Seasons, 'Spring' (1746)

JAMES WATT (1736-1819)

engineer and inventor

◇◇◇◇◇◇◇◇◇◇◇◇◇◇◇◇◇◇◇◇◇◇◇◇◇◇◇◇◇◇◇◇◇◇

I think that I shall not long have
anything to do with the House of
Commons again – I never saw so many
wrong-headed people on all sides
gathered together.

Letter to his wife (1767)

GLOSSARY

a'	all
ae	one
afore	before
aft	often
agley	awry, wrong
ah	I
an'	and
auld	old
bairn	child
bane	bone

bannock ....an unleavened cake

bile .... boil

breid .... bread

brither ....brother

bummer ....a creature that makes a buzzing noise, a bee

canna.. cannot

canny..careful

cauld..cold

chiel ....young man, fellow

claes.. clothes

cled..clad

clout..cloth

croon .... crown

dee .... die

deil ....devil

denner .... dinner

ding .... deal blows, defeat

dinna .... don't

doon .... down

draff ....pig-food

drap ....drop

drouth .... drought, thirst

dunt ....blow

een .... eyes

fa' ....fall

flee	fly
fowk	folk
frae	from
freen	friend
fu'	full
gab	mouth
gae	go
gang	go
gaun	going
gear	wealth
gie	give
giftie	gift
glaikit	playful, foolish

gree	agree
gude	good
guid	good
ha'	haw, hall
hae	have
haud	hold
hauf	half
hause	throat
heid	head
het	hot
i'	in
ither	other
Janaveer	January

kail..soup; kale

kenna .... don't know

kennin' .... a little bit

kirk ....church

kitchen... relish

lang ....long

laverock... lark

lee ....lie, to tell lies

licht..light

lift..sky

lo'ed ....loved

loodest... loudest

lowe.. flame

lowp	leap
lug	ear
mair	more
mak	make
maun	must
meat	food
mennan	minnow
monie, mony	many
mou	mouth
moyen	influence
muckle	much, large
nae	no
naething	nothing

nakit .... naked

nicht ....night

no' .... not

o' .... of

oot .... out

parritch ....porridge

pat .... pot

piece ....piece of bread,
 sandwich

pow ....head

rin ....run

shak .... shake

shoon .... shoes

siller	silver
skail	empty, spill
sma'	small
snaw	snow
soo	sow
soor	sour
stamack	stomach
stark	strong
steekit	closed
stoup	flagon, jug
tae	to
taiken	token
tak	take

thack .... thatch

thankit .... thanked

thigither .... together

thoom .... thumb

tint .... lost

toom .... empty

tyke .... dog

unca'd .... uncalled

wad .... would

wame .... stomach

wark .... work

warld .... world

wast .... west

watter	water
waur	worse
weel	well
wersh	tasteless
whit	what
winna	won't
wrang	wrong

Other titles in this series:

Auld Scottish Grannies' Remedies
ISBN-10: 1-905102-06-2
ISBN-13: 978-1-905102-06-8

Nessie
ISBN-10: 1-905102-05-4
ISBN-13: 978-1-905102-05-1

Greyfriars Bobby
ISBN-10: 1-905102-04-6
ISBN-13: 978-1-905102-04-4

www.crombiejardine.com

watter	water
waur	worse
weel	well
wersh	tasteless
whit	what
winna	won't
wrang	wrong

Other titles in this series:

Auld Scottish Grannies' Remedies
ISBN-10: 1-905102-06-2
ISBN-13: 978-1-905102-06-8

Nessie
ISBN-10: 1-905102-05-4
ISBN-13: 978-1-905102-05-1

Greyfriars Bobby
ISBN-10: 1-905102-04-6
ISBN-13: 978-1-905102-04-4

www.crombiejardine.com

5

INTRODUCTION

Scotland has had its fair share
of comedians, both professional
and self-styled, but the wit of
Scotland is not traditionally
of the laugh-out-loud variety.
Rather it is of an understated,
wry-smile type, known in
Scotland as pawkie humour. The
Concise Scots Dictionary defines
pawkie as 'having a matter-

of-fact, humorously critical
outlook on life, characterized
by a sly, quiet wit', which sums
it up very well. Alas this dry
style of humour has the
disadvantage that, unlike
the obvious joke, it can go
unnoticed. It is partly for this
reason that the Scots have
acquired a reputation in some
quarters of being dour or
humourless, but often the fault
has lain with the hearers who